WAYS OF SPEECH

Other books by the author

Growing Pains, Smith/Doorstop, 2008

Home Field, Arrowhead, 2008

The Dancing Sailors, Indigo Dreams Publishing, 2011

Say Cheese!, Rookhurst Press, 2014

Ground Cover, Indigo Dreams Publishing, 2015

WAYS OF SPEECH

ANN PILLING

Printed by imprintdigital
Upton Pyne, Exeter
www.digital.imprint.co.uk

Typesetting and cover design by narrator
www.narrator.me.uk
info@narrator.me.uk
033 022 300 39

Published by Shoestring Press
19 Devonshire Avenue, Beeston, Nottingham, NG9 1BS
(0115) 925 1827
www.shoestringpress.co.uk

First published 2020

ISBN 978-1-912524-66-2

ACKNOWLEDGEMENTS

I am grateful to John Lucas for his editorial advice and to Kate White, for reading my manuscript with such care.

I would like to thank the following people for their helpful insights into many of these poems: Joe, Benjamin and Thomas Pilling, Vera Sinton, the members of Poets Meeting, London and those of Settle Poets, North Yorkshire; my warm thanks also to Adele Geras and Jill Paton Walsh, for their encouragement whenever we meet to share poetry.

CONTENTS

for Joe

Only a sweet and virtuous soul
Like season'd timber, never gives
But though the whole world turn to coal
Then chiefly lives.

NESTING

In this matt room the only gloss is your hand
lit by the disc of a lamp as it rests lightly
on the elmy boss of your chair
I would know that hand anywhere
how the fingers feel down like long buds
rooting for warmth, splay slightly then open
into leaves that will relax all season.

Your veins are cables carrying their charge
under a thickening sea, our hands
could slough off their looseness now
be linked in boniness along one bough
house nests for thrush or dove,
useful in labour once and now again
in the longer work of love.

A MARVEL

Walking to Lissadell over wet leaves
the path slid from under me and I fell back
arms opening like wings. I staggered
fearing the bone crack.

But the wings saved me, slowing down
in smaller and smaller circles to my side
like balls dropped from a height still bouncing
like coins spun on a board.

After hard flight a bird steadies itself,
when it grips the branch its tail falls then rises.
Swifts eat, mate, sleep on the wing
when they fly to hot places.

A marvel too, to watch
how starlings scatter and mass, pluming
whole skies with smoke, to see the dip of swallows
at dusk, to their homing.

LAPWINGS

We had not thought to see them here
on a road where cars going past to the holiday homes
thump out big noise.

They are making a statement
looping the loop in a technicoloured V,
brash against sepia moorland, their blacks
sheening to purple and green, with a caramel underlay.

We stop, go very still, grope for binoculars,
while the high dance dazzles and their double call
rips up the quiet. They crash together
join, separate, join again.

Then one sinks down to the flat grass
its mate hovers and screams, hardly moving,
as if held up by a jet of air.

And from a hidden scrape something emerges and rolls about,
our lenses enlarge it to four curlicues of fluff
the kind you find under a bed
and we understand.

BIRDWATCHING FROM THE YORKSHIRE BELLE

Its newly-treacled benches have made ridges.
After an hour we stand up thankfully,
the skipper cuts his engine and we drift
into deep water under the staggering cliff.

My lenses find a gannet and its child
encircled like a painting on a plate,
a lemon head, a blue-ringed eye, a chick
battened to sheer rock by the battering wind.

In this loud hell the mother's tenderness,
preening its young, its back turned on the gale,
spears me as hard as when it splits the ocean
and dives for fishes with its dagger bill.

Was it love also when a wounded gannet
carried to safety by a rescuer
reared up and took his eye out with its beak,
as it would anything that threatened it
or threatened what it loved? It mates for life.

SPILLAGE

Wild garlic once
poured down a cart track and under a gate
and on to a lane till wheels stopped it.

A slew of white flowers. From high up
like sheep being herded through a gap
lower down like fields of coral.

When the old bridge broke
traffic was siphoned on to the highway
no one came here again.

Grass grew in the middle
seeds swelled, became bulbs, over years
the spread went mad.

It only needed time. This May
bees blunder roly-poly through the blossoms, woods
are sheeted blue. An entire lane
lies deep in the fallen snow of the garlic.

RETREAT

The town stream lies flat, its banks
neatly parallel like something from a farm set
and there is no current. Did they divert the flow
higher up, making this stretch a canal?

It's too shallow for barges, I can see the bottom,
a cloth of grey leaves, thick from years of fall,
then a twig floats by at snail's pace
and disappears under some houses. So something is happening.

In the nuns' garden I trudge
down sodden paths, November sludge
has dulled the very squirrels and all life
feels spent. But look! Before the black drops over us

that branch of small white berries, a single rose
on its long thorn, the trailing fingers
of a shrub that has flowered again and by my feet
three pinky heads of All Heal, that we call valerian.

TWO POSTCARDS

'Castle Drogo' lurches up out of the Teign Gorge
like 'Slate Rocks' by Barbara Bodichon. In both images
sky is squeezed out, we can see
only earth and the shape of the earth,
green breasts in long lines, flattish,
like someone lying down. When I was born
the war in Europe was dwindling
but might this big bald patch above the castle
be a place where planes landed?
What lies under those green pelts?

As a child I liked lying flat on my face
to smell the earth, digging my fingernails in,
feeling hair-fine creatures patter across my hands.
I knew even then that nothing is closer than earth is,
more reliable, more consoling; I felt
at home with it always, earth-creature
feeling its heart-beat
and the beat of my own heart.

THE MINES ACT, 1842

A pock-marked photograph in the museum
showed Shetland ponies stumbling on to boats
herded by grey-faced crofters.

An adventure in the big salt air
with something good in their mouths to munch on
slipped in by their masters.

Did they sense a new life as the sea widened,
a warmer life in the East
where the sun was rising?

In Aberdeen they were shunted into trucks
enclosed long days in puzzling dark
rail-roaded to the mines.

Low-standing, very small and very strong,
they swapped peat carts for coal carts,
chained to them, under the earth.

I should feel gladder for the un-chained children
bow-legged with rickets, pop-eyes
staring at the camera out of cavernous faces.

Some ponies took to the life, ate good hay in clean stables,
others died like the canaries
sent down to test for bad air.

Everything is for something. The double coat
seals it from arctic cold, its ridiculous long mane
is a wind barrier.

I pass two Shetlands when I walk past the primary school.
The children love them,
they think those weeping manes are funny.

TO CAM HOUSES

From the Kettlewell road you can walk to Cam Houses,
the track was liquorice today, flat black on perfect snow,
the fields were sand dunes spiked with marram grass.
Wind had smoothed the drifts into long garments
carefully laid down and the horizon
was lined out with a scarf of thinnest blue.
The un-snowed lower fields were apple green
with a barred window of sun on one of them
and the clouds were bubbling amongst themselves
as they romped toward me across the fell tops,
foamy, a cream-white foam with a turquoise underlay,
and I said to the dog
'Rejoice in this.'

SPANIEL

She can run here, there are no sheep
and the enclosure walls are sound
only the dead lie round
Iveson, Metcalfe, Iveson again.

She circles graves and barks
town dogs bark back, her magpie coat is brash
against the tawny grass
the duns of lichened slab and urn.

Under one stone, farmer and soldier son
face east to boned-out hills
where only silence fills
the shape of words not spoken by the dead.

The son tipped bodies into pits who'd once
heaped bales, the father offered comfort but could not
be heard; they both forgot
the ways of speech, died old here and were loved.

Downwind a shot breaks birds from cover
she hares off, yelps for joy
and comes back panting, then
lies down beside the farmer and his boy,
Iveson, Metcalfe, Iveson again.

PIG MAN

He was the biggest pig man in the Decapolis
a pig of a man himself, waistless and short,
with feet that were oddly tiny. These hard-bred pigs
were destined to make him a fortune. Then
the mad man turned up.

They didn't drown, he saw them swimming
out toward the horizon, he heard
their deep pig noises floating back to him
rich and companionable, full-belly grunts
of warm-sty happiness.

He counted two thousand pigs, they were swimming slowly.
His herd had been nothing like this,
fifty at most. They multiplied in the sunlight
heading east, the way the mad man had gone
when they ran him out of town.

Pig Man grew poor, he borrowed. Friends,
that had once looked up to him, pushed off,
so he took to a cave in the desert where he was happy.
The pigs never came back. Why would they,
understanding now what he too, at his end,
would understand?

COYPU OLYMPICS

Coypu do not fling up organic mounds
like moles, or any mounds, but grazing
the young resemble little Yorkshire fells
flattish and long, and humped toward one end.

They slither down the bank and move
in tight formation over the spiked grass
snub noses white as porcelain then zoom
across clear water, crashing

into the lily pads. Their perfect glide
gives away nothing. A parent
perches in shallows and pretends to be a tree-stump.
Synchronised, they move as one towards the further shore.

On the edge of this, and in another world,
top swimmers fight for gold and silver, nations
rise and decay; downstream the poplars rattle
presaging coming cold, and different weathers.

THE BOX

(for Andreas Lubitz)

More and more now, if I approach an altar,
the glass dissolves, the East window
flows its colours together, melts
and pours outside onto a field of sheep.

Fossil slabs smoothing the chancel steps
become powder, crabs and sea urchins
curl in the sun under a roofless vault
where saints peered down and angels used to sing.

Flesh first, then skeleton, then dust, our bodies
are bone-houses for what we were and the urn
or coffin that they seal us in at death
is all our essence now.

As on a mountain. Lowered from great height,
men comb through debris for a box
that might reveal the truth of things,
why the pilot crashed his plane, and why they died.

On 24 March 2015 Andreas Lubitz, co-pilot of Germanwings Flight 9525 deliberately crashed the plane in the French Alps, killing all 150 people on board. He had been treated for 'suicidal tendencies' and declared unfit to work by his doctor, but he withheld this information from his employers.

ON ACHILL

(at a time of the breaking of nations. June 22nd, 2016)

Surfers in black skins
wait in the waves like dolmens
a soft tide creams the sand.

These pure white pebbles could,
in a full moon, light a path for babes
out of the murderous wood.

Here is the sea,
somewhere is land. Our journeys
are many, and various.

A child sends paper boats
across a pool. My car
gets ferried home on a flat belt of water.

At Calais a boy
black-skinned like the surfers
stands by his tent, its blazon
'London, my dream'.

TODAY'S PAPER

(June 17th 2017)

Inside, two pages mirror one another.
Was this clever
or was it pasted up without thinking?
On the left a charred facade, a fretwork
of long black oblongs, on the right
a lattice of photographs, some blanks.

It is too soon, too cashing-in,
to write about the fire so here I sit
in a park with pigeons round my feet.

Someone said once, avoid big themes
don't do the Holocaust, but if you must,
pluck from the Alps of hair
that single ribbon on a child's pigtail.

Money keeps pouring in, nappies and blankets,
No more donations please, we have no storage,
it will all rot when it rains, but everyone prays
in their own way. I sit here on scorched grass
not writing about the fire.

IN THE PLAGUE TIMES

i To a Tortoiseshell Cat

In these plague times I'd rather be you.
You too have your routine
but if something skews it
you simply move on to the next thing.

You chirrup when I raise the kitchen blinds,
pick delicately at your bowl
then from a window sill
observe the birdlife and inspect the weather.

If fine you might slip out and roll on the grass
all orange-gold and snowy leggings,
if cold you might watch TV
your green eyes fixed on the flashing mortality graphs.

I envy you not being enslaved by oughts,
that you don't know about death,
apart from the puzzle of a mouse you are batting about
which freezes suddenly and won't play ball any more.

ii Old Friends

I have spent the day with old friends,
dusting books and bagging up spares
for the charity shop.

If I die in this house they will all be bagged up
apart from a few signed copies
which might fetch money.

They are my life, hoarded along the years
like bed linen and china. That Yeats with its maroon cover,
Heaney had the same edition.

Wordsworth and Edward Thomas,
Keats, a Complete Shakespeare.
Take them away and my wall collapses.

In these plague times our thoughts narrow to dying.
How will it end?
How will any of us end?

It must be awful to be disposed of without ceremony,
with no-one there to remember
the daffodils or the darling buds of May.
No-one to read 'Lights Out.'

iii Non Microwaveable

Where did I leave my tea? This house is too big,
I know that, now I am having to clean it.
In these plague times Helen can't come
so it's me for the bucket and mop.

What do people miss most?
Being hugged? Bagging their last Munro?
I most miss Helen. Singing that hymn
has not, so far, made drudgery divine.

Three rooms done and still no tea.
People think more about death these days
and about the hereafter. Might heaven be the place
where all my missing mugs of tea are?

Acres of time and we're wasting it
though some practise 'thisness',
focus for hours on the unique properties
of a kitchen chair. Others sniff flowers.

I am making a list of curious facts.
1 'The duration of this lockdown
is non microwaveable. Like the mourning process
it cannot be hurried along.'
2 'Welsh-speak for microwave is 'popty-ping''.

iv The Gather
(BBC 4)

July in Cumbria and they are bringing
five hundred Herdwicks off the fells
to the home farm, for shearing.

It's a wide valley. The lower slopes,
a bright, almost chemical green,
slant down in symmetrical pleats towards the Esk.

This same bright green drapes a white boulder
which suddenly starts to move. 'Star, Fetch on!'
Andrew stabs with his horned stick as the sheep climbs higher.

Five men, one girl, and twenty dogs
fan out over a waste of stony acres
Scafell and Scafell Pike, Esk Pike, Broad End.

As the mist burns off they look up,
the fell heaps over them, like a granite wave
that is rearing skywards before crashing down.

The camera glides silently. On ancient trods
everything narrows to a single line, the dogs
sleek after stragglers like rats.

In these plague times we need places to go in our minds.
Kate sits in a bluebell graveyard, Val
breathes in the sea, at Harwich and Hythe.

I go walking in Eskdale with Andrew
in the big silence, which feels
like one long, sweet note of music.

SPRING REUNION

Did you notice
that nobody spoke of the future, how grandchildren
threaded our chat like maypole dancers
with their ribbons of triumphs and sleepovers?

Did you notice
how cancer was kept in the wings
how stroke and second childishness
lay in long grass on the very edge of the field?

Did you notice
how brollies went up the minute the sky darkened,
filling with aeroplanes
forbidden to land?

CASUALTIES

Last week we had a tree cut down so Steve next door
could see the hills from his bed. Sometimes Anita
pushes him up the lane, his face
is a horrible fawn colour.

I'm missing the tree though our fruit bushes
will do better now and there were no nests;
the birds, at a stroke,
lost their year-round cover.

Today's casualty was a fledgling thrush
the dog had played with; it sat on the lawn
for hours after she'd gone so I cupped it,
set it head- high in a bush, but it died.

I can still feel its warmth, how my fingers stroked
the slowing throb of its head, lovely thing,
pale breast with the freckles beginning,
faint lines on its wing.

In the sycamore
a blackbird is singing. Steve in his window
watches the hills go down. Bars of shadow
lattice the evening grass.

WEEPING ASH

It died quietly in the night. If there were death throes
the gale swallowed them; and it fell with care,
sideways on to a holly tree which soon bounced back;
we can see the hills now and we have more light.

I will miss all of it, its witchy branches, its long hair,
its stubborn refusal to leaf until spring
had all but passed into summer. Only then
did its long black fingernails unfurl to green.

The logs, stacked up in chequered rows against a wall,
will last several winters. Ash burns well.
In the dark months we can hutch up close, warm
our hands at its flame

as those we have loved warm us
when we remember them.

PRACTISING

That dent in your pillow is the book
which slipped from my fingers when I fell asleep;
you were in the next room, coughing your way through the
small hours.

I am tidier on my own with my clock and my radio
my nightly pills, and I have all the bed;
if the cat comes I can sleep at a diagonal

feel it curl up behind my knees, picture its perfect oval.
I'd like a tail of my own to wrap round me,
thread under my forepaws, end at an ear.

Those *in utero* scans of babies show perfect enclosures
of frog-like shadows slowly firming up
to exit as *homo sapiens.* I'm practising going inwards.

But you can't practise for someone you love dying.
I'm glad I'm awake, my dreams last night
were too filled with people crying

and it's good that today is not bright,
that the house shakes under the wind.
I can practise curling up while rain bashes the glass
and the sea rules off the horizon with a steel blade.

DAUGHTER-IN-LAW

While she empties the house he sits in a corner
scrunched up like something flattened for the bin men,
when she shows him a tea-set his eyes slide sideways.

She remembers it, brought out for special people,
its stubby bowl and its stubby jug, brushed steel,
brought out for her. He feigns sleep.

She sorts and bags till the yard is smudged with rain,
windows blurred by a fug in the warm room;
he has not moved or spoken since they came.

She rubs a hole in the glass, they still
hang shirts in the backs where he played cricket,
stumps chalked on the factory wall.

This and the dark scullery, milk
kept cold in the cellar head and his mother
sweeping and sweeping the yard when his father died,
how her young self begged the old woman to come inside.

He drives them away without looking back
and with never a word to his wife.
Death cuts differently now, he's the one
who keeps sweeping and sweeping the yard.

BICYCLE

I am seven and in The Backs behind the houses,
an oily alley, pig bins at one end.
My father, sent out by my mother, grouses,
pushing a blue bicycle, the cast off from a friend.

His hands, big as cabbage leaves, steady
my little bum, the shiny saddle noses
my inside thighs, my buttocks clench, we're ready,
until I squeak 'Not yet!'. He pauses.

'Cowardy custard' Frankie hisses
through next door's fence. My father's face could kill.
He roars him into silence, then he whispers
'Get on again, my pet, 'You're doing well'.

After three goes I'm airborne. Never again
such sweetness between us, but I loved him then.

BLACK BARN

Its glory was the bales, fat ingots stacked
by giants. Uncle Reggie lugged one out
and made a hole for us to wriggle through.

But there were mice so we jumped off
with big owl whoops, pinching our pixie noses
like beginners in the deep end, then a rat

sleeked past, somebody screamed and there stood Reggie
like Vulcan with his hammer in his hand.
We froze, nibbled on crisps, fondled

a kitten that had snuck in after us
till the coast was clear. Then came the games again,
all that long afternoon, I can still smell it.

Nothing else mattered, parent, sister, brother.
We were gods. We knew that we would live for ever.

PAINTING BY NUMBERS

I made it from a kit, holed up for weeks
in the unused middle room. My father took it
had it framed secretly in Boots, I never once
smudged it or crossed the lines, I was so neat.

A princess feeding birds. When the birthday came
I chose blue paper, laid out scissors, string
slipped in my card, parcelled it up. The birds
sang to my song. It was the loveliest thing.

She reddened when she saw it, looked away.
I watched, I saw her small mouth twisting queerly,
I did not understand. My father said
'It's for you, my love, Ann made it specially.'

In time I saw how you perfected dying
and wished that you had been as good at lying.

SPINKS AND CO., CHILDREN'S OUTFITTERS

There was a rocking horse and a device
with sliding parts that measured feet. Miss Spinks
all bust and heels went round the shop
with boxes, party blues and party pinks

and browns for school with soles like tripe.
My satchel smelled of apples, white
as milk was my new rubber and its corners
sharp as the Venus pencils which that night

our father honed to needle points. I stroked
the badge on my left breast and traced the words
God Giveth Increase. All so long ago.
Now the cold creeps, mist nudges, birds

gather on wires, children skip down the hill
and I skip with them. I am skipping still.

HAIR

Jane, with an armoury of grips and pins,
puts up her hair and hears her mother singing
from somewhere in the past. Her head
is being towelled dry.

Ringlets tonight, for next day's birthday party;
her locks are wrapped round little pegs and bound
with bandages made wet with sugar water.
Under Gran's hair net, Jane weeps into her pillow.

Her father did school plaits with mean precision
each bow of equal size, the two braids pulled
to an even tightness, both sheered off at twelve
for the page-boy look, soft perm inside a helmet

at Mitzi's *salon*. Then the bee-hive 60's, Jane
got married in a bee-hive, lugs and lumps
to be combed out for more back-combing. Children
ended all that. Her hair fell down her back

for years and she was loveliest. Then the thinning,
hair scraped into a hasty rubber band
tendrils like sea-weed round her puzzled face.

Jane, with her armoury of grips and pins,
puts up her hair and hears her mother crying
from somewhere in the past.

JIGSAW

Sometimes I take the lid off the past
and slot it together like a jigsaw
the plywood pieces snap neatly into place
papered with coloured pictures and drawn
with the clean lines of a Ladybird book
our home, our village, our mother.

Some jigsaws weigh heavy. Stuck on a board
and varnished they can make a useful tray
framed up, a picture.
Hang it somewhere, view
the finished product. See
what the past is doing.

Is it my eyes or is the daddy
leaving the house with a suitcase?
Why have the children
been sent to the park to walk Pat?
why is the mummy crying?

MEMORIES

Always, late in the day,
they sidle back when I think
I have escaped these tormentors.

One props the door open
the rest stream through and settle
around my bed with their ruined

faces, their graveyard smell,
mutter things I can't fathom.
No-one escapes this, Socrates

prayed to forget and not
to remember. Come soon, day,
with your birdsong and children, soon.

TRAFALGAR

(for my mother, 1916–1963)

The square is round today, it swells with memory;
the fountain dishes burst, water pours over the pavings
and sweeps me to your feet on the steps of the National Gallery
perky in your pink coat.

I say 'Do you like the Blue Hen?' You chuck back your head
and shake with laughter. I don't understand.
Is this ridicule or joy? I want to tell you
that your grandson's taken silk. You tuck your arm in mine.
'Let's go and say hello to the Murillo.'

His 'Peasant Boy Leaning on a Sill' brims with love.
I had forgotten how small you were, you reach right up
and cup my face in your hands. You kiss my mouth.

OLIVER

There is no-one I know in this play
they are all sixth formers with perfect teeth
though I once knew the aunt of the Third Soldier.

Oliver in his tin-foil armour
named after Olive who died,
he's got her curly hair and oval face.

The front row is all groupies. At the end
parents carry their children away like trophies
no love pulls fiercer than this.

At our school plays I always looked for my mother
my eyes a searchlight sweeping the heads in the hall
till I found her.

Nothing existed then
but that indestructible rope along which I hauled myself
hand over hand till I reached her.

BROMLEY HOUSE

Its name belongs to the South, I see
lush fields, posh cars, but Bromley House
squatted like a toad in a cellar
in a corner of grubby East Lancashire
and people went there to go mad.

Was it mad though
to sit at the gates of Bromley House
and direct all the traffic the correct way to the M6?
Was it mad
to stare at the sky all day and not want to come in
when the stars thickened and made you want to gather them?
Was it mad
to throw yourself into your mother's grave
and eat the earth that covered her
because you loved her so?

At Bromley House
they'd let people go free till they got too mad
then they'd lock them away in thick-walled rooms
to weep for their dead mothers
for the sky
for the unpicked stars.

EXQUISITE PAIN

When a shoddy dentist drilled on a raw nerve
when a Bakelite plug broke up in my hand
and sent me flying across the room
when I saw you lying on that rug.

When a cold probe laid me open with its platypus beak
when it parted my labia
and tweezers fished for something deep inside
when I tried the kiss of life on you.

When they ruptured my waters with a hook
when my son kicked his way out with spiked heels
and I wouldn't stop bleeding.

When they drilled a neat hole in your skull
when they ringed it with purple
and I saw your pulse throb like a baby's fontanelle;
when your eyes turned into two white slits
and we had to ring Daddy.

WHEN

When she wouldn't get out of bed
When Daddy plaited our hair
When we had no clean knickers
When there was no tea
When she said she was Mozart.

When she took happy pills
When she hoovered the lawn
When she ironed all night
When she went for our Kay with the breadknife
When she said she was Christ.

When she sang very loud at the doctor's
When she swallowed the tablets
When the hospital told her she'd been a bad woman
When Johnny was drowned and she said that his mother
    deserved it
When she said she was God.

When she walked down the street with no clothes on
When they opened her skull
When our David came home
When he smelt the gas poker.

When no-one could wake her.

CHRISTMAS

The door was locked so I rapped on the upper glass.
David came out of a room
and stared at me but wouldn't let me in.

So I made funny faces, wiggled my hands and mouthed
'Cheer up, it's Christmas, nearly,' making the pane all steamy.
'It's Mummy,' I read his lips, 'I think she's dead'

and the phone on the big hall table looked very very red
and the plastic lilies were furred with dust and the gas
swirled like a sea-fog over the carpet moss.

'How's your mother?' a woman asked me the very next day,
there was nothing to eat in the house and I'd gone to buy bread.
A band played 'Away in a Manger'. 'She's fine,' I said.

A LOST TOY

The dog loves this one, an orange gobstopper with spikes,
a thing giants might play with, its rope handle
helps weaklings make big throws

but we lose it in lumpy grass
uncut since the rains when they shifted
the ewes to higher pastures.

I quarter the field like a policeman in big wellies
with a probe or a metal detector, I feel like an extra
from *Midsomer Murders*

looking for answers in woods or on towpaths.
Where is the body? I'm thinking already
of school railings cluttered with flowers.

Then something orange pulls my eye down
to a mesh of twigs but it's only
the strew of a picnic, squashed tins.

We trail home, she's hungry, walks fast.
Then a smell sends her burrowing,
her tail flaps wildly, she crunches on something.

MARBLE BOY

(at the tomb of Lord Henry Manners, 1884–1894)

The grave clothes
flow over him like water,
after nine years
his colours drained away,
he is a fine-boned boat alone on a shore.

His tomb
lies sits uneasily with the rest, its high gloss
jars with the flaking Tudor faces.
His mother smoothed the folds so sheer
the body shows through.

First a death mask,
face oiled, nostrils strawed, then plaster
patted onto the Botticelli lips.
When peeled away she started shaping
her parfit, gentil knight.

I run my fingers
down the flowings of his shroud
trace the lines of his feet, crossed like a crusader's,
and I kiss his face.

It is no colder
than others I have kissed, less shocking;
and the body is perfect, no one has carved their name.
In the glow of evening it is flesh coloured,
making death easier.

AT THE LAKE

Under a tree there were bowls
of white and yellow petals hiding
a sandy grain of ashes,
only a spoonful, there were many of us.

Take one, said the widow, Then
we will all have a share of him.
I couldn't look at you, you never want
to know about dead bodies.

He was Irish and a military man,
he had asked for Danny Boy
and for a piper; skeins of notes
unreeled themselves over the lake.

We gathered on the shore, his ashes
made long loops on the mud under the water
while birds were weaving patterns on the sky
blurring, becoming smoke.

The summer's gone and all the roses falling
'Tis I, I who must bide and you must go
But come ye back when summer's in the meadow
Or when the valley's hushed and white with snow.

If you go first, I have to tell you now
I do not plan to share you. Ashes
are my familiars, how they weigh so heavy
in box or jar, how they look like cat litter.

'Should I take this?' said a stranger.
When I gave her my bowl I saw
a smudge of ash inside. I should have cleaned it
then gone to wash my fingers in the lake
it was a part of him.
But I let it go.

THE DIVER OF PAESTUM

Night wraps its cloths round me
weaving absolute dark. Something screams in a field,
wings brush my window.
I think of people I love, and about the dead.

Are they at rest or do they tunnel like moles,
their webbed hands shovelling back the earth
as they snout blindly for sex, and food,
for shafts to admit the necessary air?

Do they think of us ever or do they float
in the shape of stars on their round black lake
then gather on its shore to watch
for the latest beautiful young man,

brand-new from earth, poising himself to slice
its waters, as the dark flood rises?

AFTER THE FUNERAL

After the funeral we walked on the headland
in un-fierce end of summer sun
where butterflies were

where caterpillars tigered black and gold
threaded the grass, where bees
found the last sea pinks unerringly, and fed.

Three heads in a line
a man and his daughters, faces
twisted like roots against grief.

The sea was a ridged silver, the blue air
scored white with wings. Friend of our life,
if this is all there is then it is beautiful,
the earth is beautiful, if this is all there is.

SAILING TO BELFAST

This is your sea, these are your crested waves,
blue veined today and the sun shining.
You crossed to England first as a young girl
shepherded off the Liverpool boat
to a train that wriggled along the coast
and rattled you to your boarding school.
Today these water-colour smudges
are yours, the hills of home.
I love your joy as the land gets nearer.

If you die first I will write on your stone
'How exciting!' I want
your calm delight to become mine too, your acceptance
of life's sorrows, your steady sense
that there is good beyond them.

SET BOOK

Those two girls, Constance and Sophia Baines,
have equal shares in 'The Old Wives' Tale',
my comfort blanket between Leeds and London.

Their story runs from birth to death,
sexy Sophia, mild, incurious Constance,
which one of them was me?

I'm saying 'was' not 'is' because I'm old
older than those two girls were when they died
one childless, the other wounded by an ingrate son.

Name three important themes in Bennett's book,
explain your choice,
what have you learned from them?

How one false move in youth destroyed a life,
that blood is thick and always outweighs water,
about compassion.

CORRECTION

(a reply to 'Warning' by Jenny Joseph)

No, to be old is to be more fragile, every morning
I take my tea in the same white cup
and its brown hair line sighs a little, cracking
that little bit more as I fill it up.

Soon it will be two eggshells in my hand
and treading on eggshells is how it gets to be
as the years increase. I for one would not offend
by stealing someone's flowers, they might pull a knife on me.

I don't want to grow fat, I did that in childhood.
If people look at me I'd like them to see
something time has improved, something good,
a sapling grown to a dignified tree.

And I don't want to hoard things, leave clutter behind,
what I care about now is the life of the mind.

THE ROCKS

These are ordinary rocks
clumped in twos and threes along the shoreline
blue-black, not smooth enough for the heads of seals
or sharp enough to be the spines of sea monsters.

Mornings a blackbird pulls worms from the grass
they escape sometimes, springing back like rubber bands,
it's a young bird, blue-black like the rocks,
and the skies have been marvellous, a different show every day.

I like this plain house, its blue and white, the way
the sun shimmers it up into a floating space
a space I could pass through and then re-enter,
re-enter for ever, until it is over

when the light becomes the dinning of the surf,
the light that I too am becoming
as we all join,
the light and the sea and the blackbird singing.

IRONING FOR ENGLAND

Up our street there's a woman who irons for England,
I've never seen her but there is hard proof
through her front window. First, a permanence
of folded linens on a chest
with heavy legs then a serious, cleanly board
flower-sprigged, always set up, a Pyrex jug
of bluish ironing water, sleeve-board, flex
coiled neatly round like a ship's rope
in the place where she must stand. The iron itself
is always cocked for action, poised
like a rocket on a launch pad sniffing the sky
and champing to be off.

I think
that those who iron, like those who dust, should take
the highest order in celestial ranks.
Heaven must be hard work with all
those goffered frills of martyrs to be done
the ruffs of the angelic choirs re-crimped
before the airing and the putting on.
And this does not begin to comprehend
the highest task of all, the eternal pressing
of the divinest garments into folds
both complicated, and immaculate.

HOME AT LAST

(after Billy Collins)

You must climb twenty seven steps to reach
the private chapel of St Chad
and I climb slowly
because of my left knee.

Near the top you can rest against a balcony
and look down on people's heads,
the shiny ones are like ball bearings
in a slowed-down game of bagatelle.

Most people go no higher but peek at me slyly
now sitting above them, facing an altar
with its stylised gold and silver angels
apparently adoring a bishop's mitre.

I like it here, I am enjoying myself,
it is warm for a cathedral and very light,
I can hear the choir rehearsing an anthem
repeating heavenly words again and again.

Jerusalem they sing, then *Peace* and then *Eternity*.
'Too loud!' (Choir Master)
'You are flat!' (Choir Master)
'That's perfect.' (God).

I have decided that this is heaven,
light, warmth and the most delightful music
below me, above me, around me,
and I'm not even hungry.

From now on, no need either, for endless prayers
that sometimes get the most peculiar answers.
I have arrived
at the place I have prayed for all my life.

ORDINARY TIME

(Malachi 4.v2)

In Ordinary Time the altars
are covered in green cloth, the church
feels like a darkened theatre where a child
waits in the wings to be born.

In Ordinary Time the grass looks dead
the land sucked dry, the trees
shut down for winter, nothing moves
under this sullen earth.

What is ordinary?
Are swallows ordinary, or bees, or seals
that will chase a stranger up a sheer rock face
to guard their young?

The child is not ordinary
lying like seed in a winter field
among all waiting things.
May the sun rise soon. May he come soon,
with healing in his wings

FIRST COMING

Lovely boy, again it is your first coming
and I make notes, guests, lists, the tree
while you in that calm womb of hers
wait patiently to be set free.

You know already that your time is short
for all your works of love, gnarled limbs made straight
blind eyes unsealed and the nine lepers leaping
on, on along the road and out of sight.

I want to be the tenth who gave you thanks,
who clasped your feet, looked in your fabulous face,
thanking you now for all that is to come,
the cross, your works of love, your work of grace.

FOR SALE

(for Christine)

How old is this house? There is no date stone
no clue carved into the timbers of the rooms
though the doors suggest they were small people
who built it on a slope of tufty grass
by a river where today I watched a dragonfly
lay its blue bar across a lily pad
like a finger against lips.

I had forgotten
how sunlight blinds you when you go indoors
and the dark of the house came at me,
shadows wrapped themselves round my head like cloths,
like garments that had been inhabited over and over,
like the hands I clapped to my cheeks, each life line
familiar from birth.

That tree by the water has been many things
over the years, a man with angels' wings,
St Francis holding a small animal.
When wind sifts the poplars its head nods,
arms tighten. Joshua saw the man at once,
children see faces in the massing clouds
when all we see is clouds.

It has grown tall, its branches have gone haywire,
it is too wide for its height. I keep dreaming
about toe-nails growing too long, piercing the ends of shoes,
about hair too lumpy to be combed free,
and I have been afraid here for the first time;
I had not expected to start fearing death
when all is so familiar.

You and I know about death,
sorrows have touched us both in this house,
things too sad for a perfect day like this
and it feels lonelier, with no-one left
to trim the significant tree that is sometimes pitiful
with its loose hands on the shake and the creature it cradles
grown helpless too.

The house we have loved is going. But everywhere
clustered like bees are memories and their sweetness,
the little chair and the bath toys, the stick people
who walk through the visitors' book. We have both
been children here and pilgrims but going backwards,
to spend plain days watching for the otter
knowing the place for the first time.

ABOUT THE AUTHOR

Ann Pilling's poems have won prizes and been commended in numerous competitions. Among them are the Cafe Writers Poetry Competition, the Faber/Ottaker Competition, the Jack Clemo Poetry Competition, the Troubadour International Competition, and the Yorkshire Open Poetry Competition. In addition, her poems have been commended at Bridport and Teignmouth and twice in the National Poetry Competition.

Her work has been widely published in magazines including Acumen, Envoi, The North, Resource, Scintilla, Smith's Knoll, Staple and Yorkshire Journal.

She lives in the Yorkshire Dales which she calls 'the country of my heart'.